JOURNEY FROM A TO Z

WITH

Teacher Judy

BY JUDY LYNN OHLROGGE

TANDY BOOKS

Journey from A to Z with Teacher Judy
An alphabetical and animal-filled adventure
Copyright © 2020 by Alex Tandy. All rights reserved.

Published by Tandy Books
tandybooks.com

Written by Judy Lynn Ohlrogge and Alex Tandy
Book Design and Creative Direction by Ryan Scott Tandy
Illustrations by Alfonso Lourido
Cover Lettering by Cristina Vanko

Library of Congress Control Number: 2020919878
ISBN: 978-1-7355771-0-4

Printed and bound in the United States of America by Bang Printing
Sustainers' Edition, 2020

This book is dedicated to my mother,

Teacher Judy, the woman who started and inspired this work.

Join me on this alphabet journey.

You'll learn each letter in a hurry.

Don't be scared, let's dive right in.

Now, where shall we begin?

A is for Arthur the aardvark,
the friendly monarch.

B is for Ben the busy bee, buzzing around his favorite tree.

C is for Chanel my cat,
who's wearing a
fashionable red hat.

D is for Dior my dog,
who takes cute selfies
for his blog.

E is for Eddie the elephant, whose trumpet sounds loud and triumphant.

F is for Freddie the fish,
who is eating a delicious
pasta dish.

G is for Gaby the ghost,
who is eating tasty
jam on toast.

H is for Henrietta the hare, who much enjoys combing her hair.

I is for Izzy the iguana,
who likes to travel
to Tijuana.

J is for Julie the jellyfish,
who is making her very first
birthday wish.

K is for Kendra the kangaroo,
who hops around to chew
and chew and chew.

L is for Leo the llama,
who always calls home
to his momma.

M is for Morris the mouse, peeking out from his little brick house.

N is for Nelly the nightingale,
who sings the most
beautiful tale.

O is for Otto the otter,
who loves to play
in the water.

P is for Percy the pig,
who enjoys eating
the ripest fig.

Q is for Quincy the quail,
who always prevails
to deliver the mail.

R is for Rodney the rooster,
sitting on his perch.

S is for Sydney the spider,
who is on his way to church.

T is for Toby the tiger, climbing to the tippy-tippy top of Mt. Eiger.

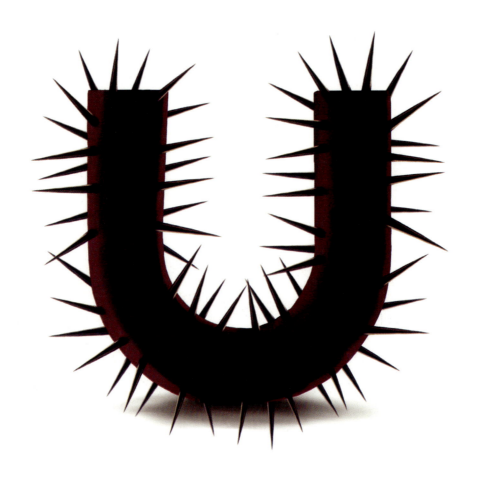

U is for Ulysses the urchin,
the greatest captain
of the wide open ocean.

V is for Veronica the vulture,
who created a mighty
and wonderful sculpture.

W is for Willie the whale,
who likes to show off
his big blue tail.

X is for Xavi the xolo ("show-low"), who scores goal after goal after goalllllllllll.

Y is for Yuri the yak,
who can carry a
mountain on his back.

Z is for Zelda the zebra, catching some z's at the end of the long, long trip.